GETTING TO KNOW
THE U.S. PRESIDENTS

WILLIAM McKINLEY

TWENTY-FIFTH PRESIDENT
1897 – 1901

WRITTEN AND ILLUSTRATED BY MIKE VENEZIA

CHILDREN'S PRESS®
A DIVISION OF SCHOLASTIC INC.
NEW YORK   TORONTO   LONDON   AUCKLAND   SYDNEY
MEXICO CITY   NEW DELHI   HONG KONG
DANBURY, CONNECTICUT

Reading Consultant: Nanci R. Vargus, Ed.D., Assistant Professor, School of Education, University of Indianapolis

Historical Consultant: Marc J. Selverstone, Ph.D., Assistant Professor, Miller Center of Public Affairs, University of Virginia

Photographs © 2006: Allegheny College Archives, Wayne and Sally Merrick Historic Archival Center, Pelletier Library: 10; Art Resource, NY/Scala: 26; Corbis Images: 3 (Bettmann), 6 (C. H. Graves), 24 (Rykoff Collection), 30; Getty Images/Hulton Archive: 8; Library of Congress/Kurz & Allison: 12; North Wind Picture Archives: 19; Ohio Historical Society/Courtney Collection: 14; Stock Montage, Inc.: 20, 32; The Image Works: 31 (Ann Ronan Picture Library/HIP), 28 (Roger-Viollet/Topham); By permission of The Wm. McKinley Presidential Library and Museum, Canton, Ohio: 18.

Colorist for cover illustrations: Dave Ludwig
Colorist for interior illustrations: Andrew Day

Library of Congress Cataloging-in-Publication Data

Venezia, Mike.
  William McKinley / written and illustrated by Mike Venezia.
    p. cm. — (Getting to know the U.S. presidents)
  ISBN 0-516-22629-0 (lib. bdg.)   0-516-25405-7 (pbk.)
  1. McKinley, William, 1843-1901—Juvenile literature. 2. Presidents—United
States—Biography—Juvenile literature. I. Title.
  E711.6.V46 2006
  973.8'8'092—dc22
                              2005012096

President William McKinley at his desk in the White House

William McKinley was born on January 29, 1843, in the small town of Niles, Ohio. He was the twenty-fifth president of the United States. For years, many historians thought William McKinley was just a so-so president. Recently, though, many experts have changed their minds.

Today William McKinley is thought of as a president who really knew what he was doing. He has been given credit for helping bring the United States into the twentieth century as an important, modern, and powerful nation.

Even if some historians haven't been sure about President McKinley, the people of the

United States in his time certainly were. They seemed to love him. William McKinley really enjoyed meeting people. He was often seen greeting citizens and kissing babies. William was proud that he could shake hands with as many as fifty people a minute.

William McKinley's birthplace in Niles, Ohio

William McKinley was born in his family's home above the local grocery store in Niles. While growing up, William liked to play soldiers with his friends. He also enjoyed marbles, hide-and-seek, ice skating, and swimming. His mother said the only difference between William and other boys was that her son was more serious.

William had five sisters and three brothers. They all had chores to do, like chopping wood, driving the family's cows to pasture, and bringing groceries home.

An illustration of an iron foundry in the 1800s

The McKinleys didn't have a lot of money, but they weren't poor, either. Mr. McKinley owned and worked in an iron foundry. He ran a furnace that melted small amounts of iron into larger bars for local use.

The northeastern part of Ohio was dotted with small foundries. William learned the value of hard work from his father. He also learned how important the iron industry was to his region of the country.

William and his brothers and sisters learned reading, writing, and arithmetic in a nearby one-room schoolhouse. William's parents felt very strongly about the importance of education. When William was ten, they decided to move to Poland, Ohio, a larger town that had better schools. In Poland, William attended an academy. After he graduated, he went off to Allegheny College in Pennsylvania.

William McKinley attended Allegheny College.

William studied as hard as he could at Allegheny College. He worked hours and hours to make sure his parents and family would be proud of him. William didn't eat well or get enough sleep, however, and ended up making himself sick. He was so thin and weak that after only one semester, he had to return home to recover.

When he arrived home, William found out his father had some serious money problems. William decided to stay at home and help his parents until things got back to normal. William was sure he would return to Allegheny College someday, but he never did. In 1861, the Civil War began. The war changed William's plans forever.

As soon as William found out that President Abe Lincoln needed volunteers to fight southern rebels, he joined the infantry. William McKinley proved himself to be a brave soldier. When he was put in charge of the camp kitchen, he saved the day during one of the worst battles of the Civil War.

A painting showing the Battle of Antietam

At the Battle of Antietam, William learned that his men were growing weak from lack of food. He quickly packed a wagon full of supplies and hot coffee. Then he hooked the wagon up to a team of mules and raced through heavy enemy fire to make sure the troops at the front were well fed. William risked his life during other battles, too. By the end of the war, he was promoted to the high rank of major.

A photo of Ida McKinley as a young woman

After the Civil War ended in 1865, William McKinley returned to Ohio. By this time, he had decided to become a lawyer. He was also anxious to get into politics. He hoped to someday make important decisions that would help his state and country run smoothly.

William began his career by working for a lawyer in the big city of Canton, Ohio. He also spent a year at a law school before becoming an official lawyer.

One day at a picnic, William met a girl named Ida Saxton. Ida's father owned the biggest bank in Canton, and Ida worked there as a cashier. William was crazy about Ida. He used any excuse he could to visit the bank.

William and Ida dated for two years before getting married. During that time, William built a successful law business. He also got involved in politics.

William had joined the Republican Party. In government elections, Republican candidates usually were up against Democratic candidates. Republicans and Democrats had different ideas about how the government should work.

In 1869, William ran for the office of county prosecutor and won. Seven years later, he decided to run for Congress. Getting into the House of Representatives wasn't going to be easy for William, however, because Ohio was filled with people who supported the Democratic Party.

William worked as hard as he could to convince people to vote for him. He surprised people by showing up in every possible corner of Ohio. William's hard work paid off. He won the congressional election in 1876.

Congressman
William McKinley

William had a lot of good ideas as a congressman. He tried to make sure people who worked in the government were honest and qualified, and that they hadn't just been given jobs as favors. He supported full rights for African Americans, who were being treated unfairly in the southern states. William also strongly believed in a certain kind of tax called a tariff.

A tariff is extra money charged for goods and products entering the United States. Many products coming from foreign countries were less expensive than American-made products. William thought that if foreign goods cost more, people would buy more products made in the United States. This would help American manufacturers and workers. Congress accepted his plan, and the McKinley Tariff was passed in 1890.

This illustration from the late 1800s shows foreign goods being unloaded along South Street in New York City.

This political cartoon criticizes the McKinley tariff. Americans, represented by Uncle Sam, are shown bearing the "weight" of the tariff while rich American businessmen get "fatter."

William McKinley's tariff didn't work the way he hoped it would, though. Since American companies didn't have to compete against foreign companies, they ended up raising their prices. Soon everything from wool suits to dining-room chairs started costing more money!

William McKinley wasn't reelected in 1890. People were angry about the higher prices. William was still popular enough with Ohio voters, however, to be elected governor of Ohio in 1891. William did a great job as governor. Five years later, the Republican Party nominated him as their choice to run for president of the United States.

William ran against Democratic nominee William Jennings Bryan. Bryan was a great speaker. He traveled the United States giving powerful talks to convince people to vote for him. William McKinley tried a different approach. He stayed at home, giving carefully planned speeches from his front porch.

Thousands of people came to hear William McKinley. Unfortunately, many of them took parts of the McKinleys' house as souvenirs! In the end, though, William McKinley won the 1896 presidential election.

William McKinley became president during a remarkable time in U.S. history. The country had become settled from coast to coast. Railroads and telegraph and telephone lines crisscrossed the nation. It was easier than ever to get around and communicate. Now many restless Americans felt the United States should start expanding its boundaries and become more involved with other parts of the world.

Restos del Maine - Remember the Maine

Recuerdo de Habana

A postcard showing the wreck of the USS *Maine*

At first, President McKinley didn't agree with people who wanted to expand the country. But soon after he was elected, an event happened that forced him to think differently. On February 15, 1898, the U.S. battleship Maine exploded in Havana Harbor, Cuba. Cuba is an island off the coast of Florida.

Spain had ruled Cuba for years. Finally, in 1895, the Cuban people rebelled against Spain and fighting broke out. President McKinley sent the battleship Maine to Cuba to show that the United States meant to protect American citizens who had businesses and jobs there.

When the Maine blew up, many Americans saw it as an excuse to go to war. Even though there wasn't any proof, newspaper reporters blamed Spain for the explosion. The people of the United States became furious. Even though he hated to do it, President McKinley asked Congress to declare war on Spain on April 25, 1898.

A land battle and sea battle during the Spanish-American War

The Spanish-American War lasted for only 100 days. American forces easily won both land and naval battles. When a treaty was signed to end the war, the United States not only helped win independence for Cuba, but gained control of other Spanish-ruled islands.

The United States was now in charge of Puerto Rico, an island east of Cuba. It also gained control of Guam and the Philippine Islands in the Pacific Ocean. While all the excitement was going on, hardly anyone noticed that President McKinley worked out a deal to make Hawaii a U.S. territory. Suddenly, the United States had grown into a major world power.

The port of Hong Kong in 1900

President McKinley and Secretary of State John Hay had also noticed that other countries were starting to trade goods with China. But these nations were pushing their way into China and not respecting the Chinese government.

President McKinley was afraid Great Britain, Germany, France, Russia, and Japan might decide to close Chinese ports to the United States and keep the trading business all to themselves. He asked John Hay to write a strong message to these nations. The message became known as the Open Door Policy. It said that the United States would like all countries to have equal rights in trading with China, while respecting the Chinese government.

The United States now had enough power to influence other nations. The Open Door Policy set up guidelines for fair world trade that lasted for years.

A 1900 campaign poster for President McKinley

In 1900, President McKinley ran for a second four-year term. Everything seemed to be going pretty well in the country. There were plenty of jobs. People were proud that the United States had won a war with Spain and gained overseas territories.

President McKinley easily won the election. He looked forward to improving trade with foreign countries and dealing with other important issues. He never got the chance to do much, though. On Sept. 6, 1901, the president was greeting people while visiting a world's fair in Buffalo, New York. Suddenly, an unemployed worker named Leon Czolgosz walked up to the president and shot him.

Leon Czolgosz was captured immediately. He said he hated the government and thought President McKinley had too much power. William McKinley died eight days later, on September 14, 1901. He was the third American president to have been killed by gunshot.

An illustration showing the assassination of William McKinley

William McKinley and his wife, Ida

As president, William McKinley was faced with a ton of problems. He handled most of them wisely and decisively. Some of his biggest problems were in his personal life. Sadly, years earlier, William and Ida had lost both of their young daughters to illness. Ida became so sick and depressed that she needed constant care.

Ida was always first on William's list. President McKinley adjusted his schedule to Ida's, no matter what was going on in the country. The people of the United States loved William McKinley for being a caring, kind, and loving husband. They felt these same qualities made him a good president.